Boredom Busters for Dogs

Avoid destructive and annoying behaviors thru enrichment

Lauren Bond
Owner/Head Trainer
B-More Charming School for Dogs
First Revision

Boredom Busters for Dogs

Avoiding destructive and annoying behaviors thru mental stimulation

TABLE OF CONTENTS

Chapter 1:
Could it be boredom?

The way we think and feel about dogs is influenced by the images we have from "Lassie" and from "Lady and the Tramp" and from "Homeward Bound." Dog stories, fed to us by the media, have led us to believe certain things about our pets that are simply not true. Dogs are not as beautifully behaved in our homes as they are in the movies. Their needs are much more substantial that media portrays them. When their needs are not met, they can behave in ways that are destructive and annoying. While we are often surprised by these behaviors, I do not think we should be. They get into the garbage, they do naughty things in front of us to get our attention, they bark, whine, scratch, and sometimes even chew up our most favorite things! Why?

I believe our dogs are bored--BORED!!!

Dogs are highly energetic. They need stimulation and outlets to use that energy. They need opportunities to experience excitement, satisfaction, curiosity, frustration, joy and relief. Changes in our lifestyles, and in theirs, too, have created a huge void between the amounts of energy our dogs have and the ways they have to express themselves.

Bored Dog's Often:

Run amok at the end of the leash
Pull on walks
Stop on walks to sniff things and refuse to walk again
Jump on everyone
Bark at their owners
Bark at small animals
Bark at anything that moves
Whine when alone or when being ignored
Bring toys to their owners to be played with
Run laps around the yard
Play keep away
Dig
Pace
Have difficulty settling in one place
Groom themselves or other things excessively
Self mutilate
Destroy furniture
Destroy blinds
Destroy Clothing
Destroy Shoes
Counter Surf
Instigate games of "chase me!"
Freak out at the sight of a small animal like a squirrel
Act depressed
Demand play or attention from people
Develop behaviors that seem anxious
Over-react to little things
Get overly excited and lose all control
Act completely out of their minds
Get into the trash
Find ways to amuse themselves, often that you don't like

Boredom Busters - www.k9boredombusters.com

When is it NOT boredom:
Separation Anxiety
Medical Maladies
Aggression
Resource Guarding

I will discuss all of these possibilities, but (as my mother would always say) common things happen commonly--we will talk mostly about boredom.

Not all dogs who behave in these ways are bored. Medical conditions can be at fault. When there is a sudden unprovoked change in a dog's behavior, it is always recommended that a veterinarian check the dog for new medical conditions. Simple medical treatments that cause the new behavior to go away as suddenly as it came can save you and your dog worry and anxiety.

There are circumstances where annoying or destructive behaviors come on suddenly, but often there is an obvious cause and effect. Sometimes, change is the culprit--change in environment, change in routine, or change in person providing care. Change is unsettling and can cause issues for all of us--these kinds of changes can be made easier on your dog and if they are kept stimulated and provided with ways to burn off their energy and anxiety.

Chapter 2: Why boredom happens

Dogs have evolved to live along side humans. As our lives have changed, so have theirs; we are on the go--in our cars, at work, running the kids around, throwing together the evening meal, doing the chores, doing our errands. Most of these are happening in places where we cannot bring our dogs. So, they are at home, maybe only to get a few minutes outdoors or a few minutes of our time. We cannot let our dogs out for a run around the neighborhood while we wash the dishes or get the kids ready for bed. Our dogs no longer live on a farm in the country where they can roam about, doing dog-like things. Even 30 years ago, dogs were running around neighborhoods all day, or better yet, had a whole acre or more to explore without ever leaving home! Don't get me wrong, dogs have a much better life now then they did 30 years ago in most places. With excellent veterinary care, wonderful healthful food, prevention of pests and parasites, humane and scientific training methods and treatment, etc. Our dogs can be more healthy, be safer, even be quite posh, with designer collars from Louis Vuitton or Nascar. We can hire dog walkers, feed them all-organic food, send them to a doggie hotel or spa or even day care. But our dogs are BORED.

How does boredom impact behaviors? Dogs are experiential learners. They like to get dirty, they like to sniff and lick things, they like to follow scents around with their noses, they like to kill tiny creatures or try to, and they like to run, and chase things, and they like to bark. The life that most dogs get to lead is at best an off leash romp at a safe park, a game of fetch with a ball for 20 minutes, a run with mom or dad, or a leash walk around the same path in the neighborhood each day. Even running off leash in a big fenced yard can be boring after a while. They eventually scare off all the wildlife, the only scent left there is their own, and they have explored every inch of the surfaces. For dogs, the same or limited stimulation is the definition of boring. Once they have sniffed and peed on all the trees along their walking route, and learned all the other dogs who walk the same route, they are no longer getting any stimulation from that outing. Dogs who ARE taken to new and exciting places are often denied the chance to enjoy them because they are kept on a leash, in heel, and expected to not pull or sniff the whole time.

As a child, in my neighborhood, we would open the door in the morning, our dog Captain would leave the house and run around the neighborhood, and before we left for school and work we would whistle and he would come home. We would leave him in the house during the day and then he would come outside to play with us in the yard or run around with us while we rode our bikes. He was streetwise, and friendly, and was well known and liked in the area. And he was far from the only one!

The place of dogs in our lives has changed, from a helper/partner in ways of rural life, to a companion in urban life. We have given them healthier,safer, more posh lives, but we have taken things away from them, too. Sniffing on walks, exploring as is their nature, is not okay, banished by the notion that they should be in heel at all times. No barking or scratching or hunting or scavenging are allowed, no jumping and maybe no playing. Many dog owners in urban settings want a nice quiet companion who wants to stay inside, who only needs 30 minutes of exercise, who will be quiet in our condos, ride in our elevators, never pee in the building and who will be fine when we come home after a 10 hour day and then turn around and leave again for meetings, dates, or family obligations. Wouldn't you be bored?

Chapter 3: Exercise is NOT Enough!

Most of us don't have the physical stamina to tire out our dogs, and we certainly don't have that kind of time every day. For many of the working breeds of dog out there, 12 hours a day in the field is in their genetics and we can't compete with those hours. Hounds were meant to be out tracking and hunting in the woods, Border Collies were meant to be moving sheep and cattle over acres of land all day, Terriers are supposed to be ridding areas of rodents, and Great Pyrenees are meant to be living in the flocks in the field guarding them from predators. I have clients all the time tell me that they take their dogs out for 2 hours a day, one morning and one evening and that the dog still isn't tired even tho the owner is spent. There are several reasons for this. Dogs like to sniff and run and roll and pounce, and most people find that physically uncomfortable if they are attached to the end of the leash! Dogs also like to get into plants, under bushes, and into water where we can't or won't go with them. So they get denied a lot of what is fun about walking. Hiking can give you some simulation of a dog's idea of fun, but even then we have to keep them on leash and have them on the path with us. Running with your dog is great exercise, provided you don't trip over them and fall, and that they don't drag you into traffic, and that their joints can take pounding the pavement! All in all, exercise is great, but it has it's limitations and some potential draw backs.

I know what you are all thinking, "Lauren said we don't have to walk the dog!"

NO WAY!!!!-- That isn't what I am saying at all.

What I *am* saying is that we can be the greatest dog walker in the world, with the best trained heeler ever, and we still won't have a tired dog at the end of every day. If you are the 1 person whose dog is completely tired out by their daily walks, then good on ya!

For the rest of us, struggling to balance variable social lives, dog needs, family needs, and healthy respect for the weather, I am here to tell you that there are other ways to exercise your dog. BOREDOM BUSTERS are the answer.

This isn't just for fun either, these methods alone could probably keep hundreds of dogs out of shelters every year. It could save lives. Because......

Boredom impacts your long term relationship with your dog

Allow me to present two real life bored dog scenarios. Each with different outcomes!

Scenario 1:
Let's say that your bored terrier sits in the front window of your urban home. He has toys on the floor but he ignores them, having become

bored with them because they are always around. He isn't allowed to chase the cat so that is not an option, and he already ate dinner so the next thing on the agenda is bed. To pass the time before bed he sits in that window and watch birds or squirrels outside and when they come close to the house or seem particularly uppity, the dog barks at it. Perhaps ferociously, but at least with a good deal of passion. You, feeling like the dog-care portion of the evening is over, are trying to watch the news in the other room and can't hear the broadcast over the racket coming from the living room window. So you do what most people do, you call the dog. The dog stops barking and comes running to you. Since you actually have nothing for the dog that competes with the fun at the window, the dog soon leaves the room and returns to the window as you have returned to the newscast. If that happens every day for a couple of weeks, pretty soon the dog has stopped coming when you call, and has taken to barking at other times to get your attention. Let's say, even better, that the dog has started barking whenever it wants anything, and you are so annoyed and tired that you just yell at the dog. Because of your annoyance and frustration with the problem, you are no longer interacting with the dog in fun or positive ways, and have found yourself only yelling at the dog when it barks. You still feed it, but you don't like it very much anymore and find that you are starting to resent it's presence and demands on your time.

Pretty sad right? And while most of us would do our best never to rehome a dog, I think this would count as a pretty big red blemish against the dog were there other circumstances that made owning a dog difficult. Let's say you had to move to an apartment with this dog? Many people say they can't take the dog with them where they are moving, and that might be true, but wouldn't this behavior make it harder to get an apartment? Would you even want to try? Did you know that of the top 10 reasons why people relinquish dogs to shelters, the number one reason is behavior problems? Followed by landlord issues, and person problems? Just doing a couple of the things in this book would make such a big difference in that.

Now, allow me to present the alternate scenario using suggestions from this book.

Scenario 2:
Your dog has just come in from a walk and you want to watch the news. You know that the dog likes to watch squirrels from the window and bark and them, so you shut the window blinds, bring the dog into the room where you are watching the news and give your dog a puzzle toy to work out, after 20 minutes, you rotate a kibble dispensing toy to the dog and take back the puzzle. 20 minutes later the kibble is done, and you give the dog a bully stick to chew on before heading out for a potty walk one last time before bed. After a couple of weeks, the dog comes in from the walk, heads right into the room with the tv, and waits on the bed for

the puzzle toy to be presented. The dog quietly works the puzzle, eats dinner, chews on a bully stick, potties and go satisfied to bed. Isn't that better?

Chapter 4: Boredom Busters for Inside

For a huge variety of reasons, ranging from foul weather to apartment residences, indoor boredom busters are a must have for every dog owner. You need to be able to entertain your dog inside the house as well as outside. In this chapter you will find suggestions on how and when and where to implement games, enrichment toys, and fun challenges for your dog.

A Word on "MINE": For years I have seen people get into bouts of "Tug-o-War" with their dog over an object they want to take from their dog. This can really complicate some of the activities in this book. I have uploaded a video of the "Mine" game on our website so you can teach your dog to release objects from his or her mouth.
It is also my recommendations that you always have something to trade for the thing you are taking away. I try to never be the one to "create the vacuum of fun" for my dog. The last trade of the session, I offer something that the dog will consume and then the dog has ended his or her own session.

A word on resource guarding: If you have a dog who shows signs of resource guarding or who has a bite history, it is my recommendation that you only use toys or treats that are consumable, or that are low level for the dog. If you have a dog who guards resources from you, then only use the tools in this book that will allow your dog to finish the entire object like some of the Chewing options below.

4a: Chewing/Gnawing

Chewing: Dogs LOVE to CHEW! They like to crunch thru bones, and make things squeak and gnaw on things they can't destroy easily. The world of dog chew options has expanded to what truly can be called a buffet. There are reusable chews, digestible chews, even some chews that are dangerous. Here are some options that are safe and tend to be widely available and most importantly loved by dogs!

A note on sources: More on this in the resources chapter. But at this point, I recommend that you be cautious of anything, food especially, that is made in China. My personal preference is US sourced, and barring that, I am comfortable with food items from Latin America.

-Kongs
    The Kong Company has developed a wide variety of toys but I always find myself coming back to the original.

It is a versatile and durable toy that is easy to clean and reuse and almost every pet supply store carries them. You can use the original kong in a variety of ways. It can be stuffed with a meal and given fresh to the dog, it can be stuffed and frozen, frozen into a block of water, it can be microwaved, and most importantly, can be cleaned in the top rack of your dishwasher.

There are a variety of stuffing recipes available on the inter-web. You will find diagrams, diabolically difficult recipes, and fun pictures of dogs enjoy this versatile toy.

-Body Parts

Some people have a hard time with the baser desires of their dog to eat animal parts. However, they are some of the most simple, long lasting, and most digestible boredom busting options for most dogs. Parts come in all shapes and sizes, and are available from a variety of sources. Pig legs, beef knuckles, tendons, hocks, tails, ears, hooves, and bones. Most of these sources come in both a meat-on and meat-off option. I find that meat on tends to stink a little bit, for people with sensitive noses, but that the dogs find them MUCH more interesting them the sterilized meatless options. Still, if you are going to give your dog real animal parts, I would recommend that you keep them off the carpet or sofa until you are sure how messy of an eater you have. If you don't have a floor that is easy to clean, I would recommend that you give the meaty body parts only in a crate or outside.

The other body part option, and the one that we have found to last the longest is naturally shed deer antler. They aren't the most interesting item to chew on, but you can add to their value by burying them in your dogs kibble, or putting them in a bag with something else meaty to enhance their flavor. I have some clients who have had their antlers more then 6 months with some pretty heavy chewers.

-Bully Sticks (Pizzles) *(*Universally Loved*)*
These sticks are one of the most popular dog chews I have ever seen. The dogs love them because they are tasty, the humans love them because they don't stain anything or leave any crumbs behind. They also often don't smell bad. They come in a wide variety of sizes, widths, lengths, and prices.

-Bones
Remember earlier when I mentioned that cooked bones come in two forms, with meat or without. That wasn't the whole story. Technically they also come sterilized, without meat and without marrow. Sterilized and without marrow makes them ideal for adding your own stuffing. Since the bones are sterilized, they are basically indestructible to all the but strongest chewers, and they can be reused by washing them and adding new stuffing to them. You will find stuffing recipes and a list of safe foods in the recipe section of this book. A quick note on storage: I recommend that all stuffed bones be frozen after they are stuffed. It will take your dog longer to eat the goodies inside and it cuts

down significantly on the mess created during the eating. Fresh is fine, but will be messier and won't take as long for the dog to empty them out.

-Antlers *(*Longest Lasting*)*

These are another recently commercialized dog chew that I imagine farm dogs and avid hikers have enjoyed for some time. The companies that sell them go out and collect naturally shed deer antlers and saw them up into a variety of widths and lengths. They are hard as steel (Remember that deer use them as weapons) and they can take a good amount of chewing. I have never had a chew last as long as my dog's antler has lasted. The trade off is that they aren't super palatable or fun for your dog since they are just gnawing on them. I recommend that when your dog isn't chewing on the antler, that it be stored in the bag or container of kibble. That way it picks up the smell and dust of the kibble making it more palatable.

-Sherpa Cheese

These are a recent addition to the market for dog treats and to date I only know of 2 companies making them. Himalayan Dog Chews and Churpi Chews. These chews are literally the same the cheese that Sherpa's carry up into the mountains for nutrition. Their ingredients are cows and yaks milk, lime, and salt to curdle the milk. Then it looks like they dry the cheese for an eon. What is left is the densest, hardest looking hunk of cheese that your dog will LOVE. And they tend to spend quite a bit of time chewing on them. My dog will gnaw on it for a while, get some of it soft, lick that off, and start over again. They are a worthwhile investment for you medium sized dog owners, who have big chewers in small bodies. For bigger dog owners, it can be pricey but it is great to watch them enjoy this special snack! And because they are made of simple cheese, they are completely digestible!

-Frozen Stuff

I know most people have heard not to give chicken bones to dogs. Here is where that rule gets broken, a little. You must NEVER give COOKED chicken bones for your dog, EVER! The heat used in cooking makes the bones brittle and they are likely to splinter in to sharp shards and are dangerous for your dog to chew, swallow, or try to digest. People have really good reason for telling you to stay away from chicken bones. However, if you don't cook the bones they don't become brittle and they won't shatter into needles. So raw chicken bones, and better yet, frozen raw chicken bones are completely safe and fine for dogs. Generally the parts the chicken made available for pets in frozen raw form are necks, wings, and backs. You can ask your butcher for any other part you can think of, but those are the most popular because of their size and their meaty content. Salmonella isn't an issue for dogs, but is still a concern for us, so give your dog the bones in his or her dish, or in on a floor that is easy to clean. And be sure to wash your hands.

Boredom Busters - www.k9boredombusters.com

Having said my piece on chicken, there are many other frozen bone options for dogs. Most butcher and grocery stores sell "marrow bones" for dogs. Often these are beef legs that have been sawn into small sections. But for big dog owners, you can even ask for the whole leg bone. Companies that make raw dog food will often package raw leg bones for animals they use for food. So you may be able to find, pork, venison, bison, rabbit, duck, or beef at your local natural pet store. The companies that are US made and that I know of personally that package these items will be listed in the resources section.

-Rawhide warning
We don't recommend rawhide bones or chips to our clients. Rawhide is the dried uncured hide of cows. The trouble with rawhide is that it isn't digestible. It is molded or shaped when wet, and then left to dry. Once it is dry, a little bit of liquid, ie dog spittle, puts it right back to soft and pliable. When it is soft, the dogs can tear pieces off and swallow them. This is dangerous because as rawhide continues to absorb liquid it can expand, getting stuck in throats, stomachs, or intestines. The removal of rawhide requires surgery. If the dog does manage to pass the rawhide on their own, there is often some diarrhea associated with the indigestion.

-Plastic Bones
There has been a lot of recent (last 10 years) misinformation and scuttlebutt about the

ingredients and safety of Nylabones and Astrobones and their comrades. Basically they are made from a plastic/polymer like substance that is molded into a bone or other shape, and has an added scent or flavor. They are meant to be chewed but not eaten. They recommend that if your dog swallows a piece bigger then 1/4 inch that you "inform your veterinarian."

Nylabone brand does make some "edible" options but those aren't much safer and they certain aren't something I would want my dog to eat. They are made of rawhide, wheat, soy, cellulose, and a fair number of other chemicals and compounds that you shouldn't give to your pet. Again, these may be a great option for dogs who are simply looking for something to chew, but don't leave your dog unattended with them and be sure that they aren't consuming any of the plastic.

-Fuzzy/Squeaky/Awesome

The most frequent question we get at the store is "What toy can my dog not destroy? I need the indestructible toy." My answer unfortunately is "There is no such thing. There are toys that are more durable then others, toys that have more squeakers then others, and toys that are easier to repair then others, but nothing in indestructible."

This may come as a shock to some of you, but dogs are hunters....they like to kill things. This is why dogs LOVE squeaky toys! We should love it to because it is a humane, fun, and safe way for them to practice their hunting and killing. That is why no squeaky toy lasts very long. Having said that, there are some that are more durable then others. Tuffy Toys as a brand are surprisingly durable because of their layer and stitching style. They often manage to still to be fun to play with, even if some of the stuffing has been pulled out. In various models made by Tuffies, there may be less stuffing. The other toys that seem to be more durable then most as the MonsterPulls and the PentaPulls. Again stitching seems to be the key here, coupled with low stuffing these seem to be the most durable. Again, the fun in playing with these toys for the average dog is the ability to "kill" it.

Other squeaky toys that seem to hang in there a bit longer are those that have more then one squeaker. The Pentapulls and MonsterPulls fall into this category, but the ruler of this is the Kyjen Plush Puppies MEGA Squeak Squeaker Mat with models that have a 6 or 9 squeaker model of a snake, a raccoon with 8 squeakers, and an alligator with 15 indivdually stitched in squeakers.

Lastly, if you are handy with a needle and thread, you can purchase replacement squeakers and keep sewing them into the un-stuffed toy. The stuffing and squeaker can be re-formed into any number of toys that seem like fun to your dog! You could even make your own squeaky toys and then continue to repair them until you feel like making a new one!

Hunting/Searching:
4b: Hunting/Searching

-Hiding Dinner
    Dinner doesn't have to come out of a bowl, or off a plate. You can hide it in a variety of manners. We will talk about alternative ways to feed dinner in a later chapter, but in the meantime, for hunting there is nothing better.

-Scattering of valuable things
    If your dog has a favorite stuffed animal, or a favorite kind of chew toy, even a stick in the yard then you can play this game. I will take my dogs frisbees, his favorite thing in the world, and I will hide them around the house. He knows the word for frisbee and at the mention of it will start frantically running around searching for it. Think of this a long range or pre-staged fetch.
    If your dog is used to fetch, make a big deal of the Fake Throw, and have already placed the object far away. Sometimes I will hang it in a bush. Most dogs will look for it if you don't move to help them. This is critical, DON'T MOVE. None of that "oh, look silly, it is right there....." stuff. All of that teaches your dog to wait for you to get the object for them. If your dog is new to searching for toys, or doesn't know the names of special toys there are a few products on the market that might help. They are plush toys or tug toys that have a pocket for smelly treats or food. Hiding those will help your dog cross over from finding food to finding toys.

(EXAMPLES: Ultimate Jackpot Toy, Kong beaver with replaceable squeaker velcro pocket)

-Scent Games

Scent rules. Some breeds more then others, but truly in the world of dog, scent is king! If your dog loves the smell of vanilla, you can let them hunt for vanilla. If you dog loves the scent of kibble, hide kibble. If your dog loves the smell of cheese, hide cheese.

If you aren't interested in having your dog cleaning loose kibble out of your garage or pantry, you could always make scent tubes and hide those around the house. Scent Tubes are short sections of PVC pipe with a few small holes drilled into them. They have caps at each end, one of which is usually removable. Those tubes can be filled with anything the dog enjoys hunting for. If you have a yard or some extra space, you can bury to tube under leaves or a bush. If you are playing in the house, you can use bookcases, pillows, closets, etc. While your dog is searching for the item, you can sit back and watch. When the dog finds the tube, you can throw a party.

Nose work is fast becoming one of the favorite and cutting edge classes available to dog owners today. The act of learning to follow a scent is great for dog brains and for human exercise. It is also be fun to learn all of the peripheral skills involved. Teaching a dog to search on cue, teaching your dog to have drive and motivation for something other then food, and teaching your dog an obvious and unmistakeable indication behavior can all be great fun. Examples of indication behaviors include but aren't limited to: jumping up on the person, sitting beside the object, pulling a special hanger off the person, picking up the object, picking up a handkerchief or other object.

-Collecting things

Similar to long distance fetch. This is the game of having hidden things that the dog can retrieve all over the house, yard, or park. Tennis balls are great for this, since if they are lost they aren't nearly as expensive to replace as stuffed animals or frisbees. And you can hide multiple of them for your dog to find. The idea of the game is to have your dog grab a tennis ball, and bring it to you. When the dog arrives with the ball, trade them the ball for a cookie. Then send them to get another ball.

This is also the baseline game for teaching your dog to clean up his own toys.

-Finding favorite people

Ever wanted to train your dog like Lassie to go fetch a person? Ever wanted to name people in the house so you could pass notes or send the dog to alert to dinner or emergency? This game is great to play and can come in handy as a training tool.

First, start with the people in the same room. The Sender will need to have the dog's attention. The Reciever needs to have treats or a toy hidden. The sender says the name of the reciever, and points to the receiver. The dog turns to look at the reciever and the reciever calls the dog over and give treats. Do this several times, then extend the distance slightly. When you can send the dog across two rooms start moving the reciever just out of sight. Then move them further out of sight. Then move them into hiding, and teach the dog to go looking for them. Then use the dog to pass notes.

Eating:
   4c: Eating

Dogs need to eat to survive. And most of them get to practice eating twice a day. Why waste those opportunities to get some energy out of your dog? As mentioned in the section on hunting, moving your dogs food around or making a game out of dinner or breakfast can be a great way to build in some concentrated work time for your dog while you take care of other things.
Without having to buy anything new, you can simply move your dog's food dish to a new room or location each meal. This does require that your dog be confined or out of sight when you move it, and then releasing your dog to go find it. This simple exercise can be a great jumping off block for several other no-tools needed feeding options.
        -You can hide your dog's food around the house in small piles, or put paper plates or cups around that have a portion on of the meal on it. Placing several of these, and moving their location each meal will keep your dog working for longer and longer periods of time.

-You can also move meals into areas that aren't favorites of your dog. I encourage clients to put dinner in crates or bathtubs or even in a car if those places are scary or not fun for your dog.

* *Added Bonus** Moving meals around the area will also help keep your dog flexible and happy during mealtimes if there is a change in routine. If your dog goes to stay with a friend, or has be kenneled, or if you travel with your pet, having a dog who is flexible enough to eat anywhere off of any surface can help make change easier. It will also help keep mealtimes consistant, since your dog can eat anywhere at their regular times. This can be really important if you are dealing with illness, medication, or the need for weight gain.

Kibble dispensers:

There are several products on the market that provide a variety of levels of skill from your dog to release kibble. If your dog is eating wet food, or defrosted raw, don't despair....there are options for you guys in the next section.

Kibble dispensers are designed to make the dog work or interact with the dog in a specific way in order to have the toy pay! The simplest version of this is still the kong, although the shape of the original kong makes that an easy task.

Other products on the market include the Kibble Nibble by Premier:

The Twist and Treat by Premier

The Tug a Jug by Premier

The Genius Mike by Kong

The Genius Leo by Kong

The Chuckle and Waggle by Premier

The Atomic Treat Ball

The Buster Cube

The Kong Kibble Dispenser

The Tricky Treat Ball

The IQ Ball

Go to our website for images and a few videos of a dog eating out of these toys

 Later on, you might want to hide it in a different object like a pie plate or paper cup. More advanced dogs could have it hidden in several locations around the house. And expert dogs could be challenged with food in different objects on different levels of different rooms in different sections of the home. (I have fed my dog out of a vase on the floor, from the soil of a potted plant in a cup, off a plate on the airchair, and from the basket on my stairs, then I put a big bowl in the bathtub.) *Teaching your dog to eat in places that they otherwise consider to be scary, boring, or unfun can have the added benefit of making that place more interesting, less fear inducing, and at least less dull.

Games
4d: Games

Did you know that you and your dog can play hide and seek with each other? Did you know that you can use your dog to send notes back and forth between family members? Did you know that you can even play fetch in the house?

Depending on the size or your house and the number of valuable antiques therein, you can play a huge number of games with your dog inside when the weather is icky.

You can play tug of war.

Fishing for Pups: You can attach a string to your dogs favorite toy and make it move around the room or house by pulling at it. This is especially entertaining if you loop the string around several pieces of furniture so that sometimes the toy disappears under an object and re-appears where your dog isn't expecting it. Young kids love this game, and it can be fun to watch your dog chase something that you are moving while you sit perfectly still except for winding up the string!

Stair Mastering: I can play fetch with a soft ball with my dog up and down the stairs in my house. I close all the doors in the upstairs hallway, stand at the bottom of the stairs and throw my dogs ball up into the upstairs hallway. He runs up to get it, and brings it back to me at the base of the stairs. This is great physical exercise as well a good game for him to play.

Destructo: I sometimes help my dog destroy toys. I will start to play tug of war with him over a soft stuffed toy, and I will encourage him to rip it up. Once he gets it started I will continue to encourage him to pull all the stuffing out, and rip it to shreds. If I don't see enough enthusiasm, I will actually get on the floor and help him. My dog has actually learned to take turns pulling out "mouthfuls" of stuffing from a toy even tho I am just keeping the same handful each time.

Puppy in the Middle: I can also play keep away from my dog if I have another person. Throwing the ball or frisbee back and forth over the dogs head makes him run around and get all excited. After a couple of tosses one of us usually missed (not always on purpose) and he gets the toy. Then he gets to play with it while we start a new keep away with the next toy. This creates value for the dog because the resource is clearly valuable to you and frustration is a great motivator.

Hide and Seek: Hide and seek is best played with two people or more people although it can be played with just you and your dog.

Everyone gets loaded up with treats and starts in the same room calling your dog back and forth between the two people. When the dog is with the other person, you start moving further away until you are out of sight. As your dog gets better at this, you can start to hide before you call your dog to come find you. Then, while the dog goes to find the other person, you hide somewhere else! This is also a great way to teach your dog to pass notes back and forth, but you need to teach your dog to go look for someone that they know rather then coming when they are called. Suggestions of hiding places include closets, in the shower, behind doors, under beds, or under covers.

The number of games you can play with your dog are endless. Do you have great games you play with your dog inside? Send us an email or leave a note on our facebook page! We love to hear new ideas from our readers!

Chapter 5: Outside Boredom Busters

The great outdoors is a wonderful place for dogs. With each new day brings a new weather pattern, new scents on the wind, new dogs having marked new things, and a whole new set of animals to chase around. While the weather sometimes makes spending time outside with a dog unpleasant, there are plenty of days that you can use the great outdoors to combat boredom in your dog.

WALKING:
Walking for Potty:
A couple of times a year I get phone calls from clients who are having a hard time walking their dog and fear that their dogs housebreaking is backsliding. Often these phone calls go something like this: "She has been having accidents in the house and the vet says there is nothing wrong with her. We are spending more and more time outside, and she still isn't pottying. So I bring her back inside and she goes on my rug." Often what I discover with these clients is that the only time the dog gets to go outside is to potty. And the only walks the dog gets either by design or because of the increased time spent outside to potty, is the one meant for bathroom use. Generally, what has happened to these dogs is that their owners take them out for a walk, and wait for the dog to "do their business" and then head immediately back inside, feeling safe and

satisfied that the dog is now empty and they can get back to whatever else they need to do. Often these owners say things to me about "guessing that spot isn't what she liked" or "he is really picky about where he likes to go" or "I just need him to hurry up and go, and he seems to be dragging it out."

What has happened from the dog's perspective is this: "I want to be outside and sniff stuff, and I get distracted sometimes, but mostly I like to stay out. As soon as I potty my mom or dad takes me right back inside, so I am just holding it as long as I can. Sometimes that backfires and they take me in, even when I haven't gone, and then I have an accident."

The way to fix this is actually quite easy. Don't do any walking until the dog has gone potty. If I want to take my dog out for a nice long hike, we don't leave the house until he has gone to the bathroom.

It is as if you have to retrain your dog to think, "gosh, if I potty quickly, sometimes we go on a nice long walk." This is so valuable if you live in an urban area, where all pottying has to be done on leash. It is allows you to do a quick run out the door, request a potty, and then run back inside in bad weather, at odd times, when there is a lot going on, and it sets you up to be able to enjoy your walks with your dog when you chose to take them and make them nice and long.

WALKING FOR MY EXERCISE: I am a walker, I always have been. If I wasn't riding my bike somewhere I was walking. Walking for my purposes is distinguished from hiking, in that I walk around my neighborhood, I walk around urban areas, I walk on a paved paths.

Lots of people get dogs in the hopes that they will lead healthier lifestyles because of the dog's needs. While this is sometimes true, I think there is a lot of frustration about the difference in walking styles between humans and dogs.

When I go out with my dog to get my exercise, I have very specific expectations. I want to walk, at my pace, for my length of time, without stopping, until I am tired or we are home again. This requires a number of things from my dog. It requires that he match my pace, no faster (pulling) or slower (lagging behind). No stopping to smell things or go potty. No greeting people or other animals. Waiting at corners with me, and moving when I am ready to move. It is also nice if he stays on one side of me as I would rather not have to change the length of my striding to avoid tripping on him. This is a long list of requirements and takes a number of training sessions to accomplish perfect harmony.

This can be a great way to help keep your dog fit, but it isn't necessarily going to keep him stimulated. Depending on the dog, and his or her stamina, you might find, as I do, that I what I consider to be a long walk is just a warm up for my working breed dog. From a dog's perspective, he might as well be walking on a treadmill or on a track, for there isn't anything else to do with his brain but keep up, stay to one side, and ignore everything else.

Just looking at the sales figures for the wide variety of "no-pull/walking" contraptions out there, will tell you how much most people want this to work out. But isn't what your dog has in mind when he thinks "walk outside." Your dog wants to sniff things in the grass, he wants to roll in things, he wants to pee on trees. He wants to greet people/dogs/animals, or at least investigate them. He or she wants the Walk for Mental Stimulation.

WALK FOR MENTAL STIMULATION: This is a walk that boggles the mind of most of my clients. For whatever reason, they feel like they are supposed to walk the dog down the street in a perfect "military heel position" and that their daily walk in heel will be enough to satisfy their dogs needs. Why not run with your dog to chase the squirrel up the tree, or to scare off the bird on the sidewalk? Then go back to standing around while your dog enjoys waiting for the squirrel to come back down. Just for the record, both birds and squirrels are smarter then they look, and faster then you.

As I have mentioned in previous pages, dogs are living a less interesting life now then they ever have before. We give them less and less attention, less and less exercise, less and less dog-ness. Dogs want to run and stop to smells things, they want to change course on a whim, or a scent, or a running animal. They want to be the wonderfully in the moment, attention deficit disorder, smelly, stinky, joyful animals we love them for!

All of that sniffing, and peeing, and rolling, and running, and stopping, and being distracted is GREAT for your dog's brain! A dog who gets to satisfy his basic urges is a much happier dog indeed.

So, take your dog out on a "walk" and just be the anchor at the end of the leash. Just let him take you where he wants to go, follow along willingly. You don't have to accept being dragged, you don't have to be tense on the leash, but let her zig-zag, let her stop for as long as she would like, let her lay down in the grass and roll in whatever she found, let he meet people, or animals, or whatever she likes. I set a timer on my ipod, or listen to a chapter of an audiobook while out on these walks with the dog.

A note on location: In order for your dog to be interested in sniffing and rolling and marking and carrying on, you need to provide an environment that has things to sniff, and roll in, and mark, and carry on about. This often means taking the dog somewhere new every couple of days.
Try these places/suggestions:

-Go a couple of blocks further away from the house for the whole walk.
-Get in the car and drive to the next neighborhood over.

-Get in the car and drive to a really nice neighborhood with sidewalks and pretty houses to look at while your dog sniffs things.
-Drive to a friends neighborhood and walk with your friend around their hood.
-Go to a busy park with lots of people and animals and you don't have to go very far to find things to entertain your dog.
-Go to a quiet park and take a long walk slowly around.
-Go to a pick-up soccer game or beer league softball game and watch while you walk.
-Go to a school and watch the high school sports teams while walking around.
-Find an outdoor concert or art event and walk there.

In my area of the mid-atlantic, there are so many things within a couple hours drive. We can get to the beach, and the mountains, and the parks all in one day, so I take advantage as often as I can. Just taking the dog and walking the boardwalk is great for him. It is fun, people love to see him, and he often gets a french-fry or two in the process! Going to the mountains is often a solitary activity, we don't see many people, but he can follow the trail of whatever deer or possum he can find.

HIKING: My husband and I do a lot of hiking and camping and exploring of parks and areas around our home state. And we love to take the dog with us. Some parks don't allow dogs, and almost all parks require that dogs be on leash the whole time so they don't harass or kill wildlife. I like to keep my dog on a european or 10 way leash so that I can have my hands free and he can sniff things without pulling on my shoulders. This also might be the one place that I would consider using a retractable leash, but only maybe. I also can decide to stop and let him roll in something or get a drink from a stream while we are out there. Nothing is more fun for an urban dog then getting to roll in deer urine or getting to chase a butterfly. And even a short hike can be tiring after all the sniffing and peeing and hills.

BIKING: Biking is a great way to get your dog tired out physically, but it can also be fun mentally for them. Places where you can go biking are often places where your dog will want to sniff and mark and explore new scents. If you aren't a great biker see if you can enlist someone who loves to bike to take your dog attached to them. There are now devices that attach to your bikes rear frame and to a harness on your dog that will keep your dog behind your pedals and away from the bike enough that they won't trip you up.

SWIMMING: Depending on your breed of dog, you might not have choice about this. I know several golden retrievers and labs who manage to find water to play in, even if they are in the middle of the desert. Swimming can be fun for dogs, but it can also be scary and dangerous if your dog doesn't know how. My dog would drown in an instant if he went into water over his head, but he will splash around in a shallow stream happily chasing fish or reflections or floating leaves. If you have a dog who loves to swim be sure that they don't get themselves too tired to make it back to shore. Also chlorine isn't great to dogs so your neighbors swimming pool probably isn't the best place to go try this out.

If you are going to throw toys for your dog be sure that the object will float, and that you aren't in an area with lots of debris under water. You don't want your dog to tangled in branches or rope or get cut on an underwater tree while out swimming.

PLAYGROUPS: Does you area have fenced in Dog Park? Do you have friends with dog friendly dogs who have fenced in yards? Does your local neighborhood park have a basketball or tennis court you could use? Playgroups can be a great way to get some positive dog socialization. It isn't a good idea to just meet up and throw a bunch of unknown dogs together, but once you have a good group of dog friends, this can be a great boredom buster. If the dogs have never met before it is a good idea to start off the first play date by taking a walk together, with some distance between at first and then shortening the distance over the walk so that they meet and walk together in the same direction for a while before they get to play off leash. This should be the procedure for bringing any new dog into the group and is a good overall policy to ensure positive experiences for everyone. Keep the playgroups short, just like with little kids, the more tired they get, the more cranky they become.

Lastly, a note on toys. Many dogs love to play with toys, but if they are the only dog in their house, they might not be great at sharing. It is best to avoid toys in a playgroup unless those toys are present in anyone's home. And even then, it might be too precious to share and could lead to fights.

NOSE WORK: Nose work is a fancy term for teaching your dog to search with their nose for a particular scent and do a trained indication when they find it. In NYC last year, someone I knew made an amazing amount of money with her dog doing bed bug detection. She went and collected some bedbugs, taught her dog to bark when he found them, and then charged hotels and apartment buildings to come in and have her dog look for bedbugs so they could get rid of them. Nice work if you can get it! Dogs at airports are trained to sniff out contraband items at customs, and drug and bomb dogs do the same for law enforcement. It is all the same training, but rather then the danger of having explosives around or having to collect bed bugs, most nose work is done with simple scent oils like clove, birch, or vanilla.

AGILITY: Agility has gained amazing popularity over the past decade. Now there are several nationally ranked competitions in every state. If you have ever watched agility on TV or in person you know that there are a lot of different obstacles that your dog will need to be able to navigate. This can be daunting for some people because of the variety and expense associated with each obstacle. There are some cheap dog agility suppliers online, but if you are handy you can build your own. When I was doing FEMA Search and Rescue for urban disasters we used to do "Junkyard Agility" which literally meant we went to the junkyard and got all the cable spools, and fencing materials, and 55 gallon drums, and pieces of scrap wood and made obstacles out of them. Agility doesn't have to be about walking an A-frame or running thru tunnels, it can be about walking across a ladder that is elevated off the ground, or running thru a barrel, or weaving around old stop signs. The possibilities are endless and it is all about having fun!

TRACKING: Want your dog to learn to follow someone's scent around the yard? Help your figure out which neighbor borrowed your rake without permission? Tracking is a great skill for dogs, and many of them do it naturally. If you have ever owned a beagle or a hound you already know they can't go anywhere without their nose on the ground. One way to develop this skill without having to become a police officer is to plant one piece of food in every footstep. So, have someone take a step and before they lift up their toe in each step, have them put a piece of food on the ground under their foot. This will teach the dog to put their nose in the scent while eating, and will help your dog associate sniffing each footprint with fun. Start on concrete, move to grass, then only put the food in randomly. If you have a dog who is great at this game or who wants to learn more about searching for things, check around for a trainer in your area who offers a Nosework class. These classes are often linked to a competition style search game. If you have a dog who is amazing at this and needs something else to do, contact your local search and rescue team and see what is involved in training with them! Again, check the resources section of the book for more places to get information.

TOYS ON A ROPE:
Attaching a stuffed animal to a rope and using the rope to pull the toy around the yard is a great boredom buster for dogs who like to chase. The object at the end of the string can be something obvious to the dog. A biscuit on the end of a string might not be visible to your dog, but a frozen bone should be big enough. If you are going to use something edible on the end of the stick, be sure you remove the string before you dog gets to have the item. You don't want the dog to swallow string and end up in surgery.

FLIRT POLE: Sometimes also referred to as teaser stick. This is similar to a cat toy with a string on a stick, but much bigger and sturdier. Similar to putting a toy on a string and pulling it around the yard this item allows you to encourage your dog to jump out away from you thanks to the stick. There are no commercially available Flirth Poles that I know of, but we have plans on our website. You just need a stick or piece of pvc pipe, some rope, and a toy to attach to the end. It is an inexpensive item to make and can be combined with other items such as a food dispenser or piniata that would make it extra-specially fun for your dog.

SUMMER SPECIFIC BUSTERS: Summer brings all the heat and humidity and bugs to most places. So, while there are benefits, there can also be drawbacks. Dogs can suffer heat exhausting and heat stroke which can lead to seizures and death. Dogs need flea and tick and heartworm protection to avoid icky and life threatening diseases. But, if you are planning fun, structured activities for your dog, you can keep them safe, cool, and happy in the summer months while still getting out of the house!

    -Baby pools filled with water and toys (toys include frozen kongs, frozen chicken or beef stock ice cubes, tennis balls, neoprene stuffed toys, etc.)

    -Baby pools filled with just ice can be a really happy time for artic dogs like Husky's or Malamutes. To add some excitement or encourage playing in there add a couple of chunks of frozen chicken or beef stock into the ice cubes.

    -Freezing food dispensing toys or bones into blocks of ice. This presents a real challenge for dogs and will reward hard workers who stick to the task of freeing their favorite toys or those who are calm enough to wait for the ice to melt. To encourage dogs that are hesitant, you can also freeze food around the outside of the mould or inside the ice.

-Sprinklers, gentle is best. I know dogs that want to run through them as much as the kids do!

-Blowing bubbles (They make meat scented bubbles to encourage dogs to chase and pop them)

-Building a digging box and bury items in the sand for your dog. Wetting down the sand will cool it off and make it easier to get off your dog.

For me, my favorite summer boredom buster is to load up the car with a cooler and chairs and drive out of the city into the rural section of the state and find a stream to sit beside and soak my feet in while my dog splashes around. I will spend a whole afternoon reading and hanging out with him. He will spend much of the afternoon chasing fish, flying insects, or frogs. Then we often stop at the self-serve dog wash on the way home and spend our evening grilling and chilling on the back deck. I am always sunburned and he is always tired!

WEARING A BACKPACK: This is an option that almost didn't make it into the book, but I wanted to address it since it has gotten some wide-spread press in the past thanks to certain television hosts. The concept behind the backpack as a way to tire out your dog is that it adds extra weight when filled with items and that makes it harder for your dog to move around. It is akin to running with weights on your ankles or while you wear a hiking pack. The problems with the backpack are:

-that it doesn't do anything for your dogs mental exercise

-it is hard on your dogs joints and back to carry a lot of weight.They aren't built like horses for weight bearing.

-it can be an overwhelming sensation for a dog if they aren't used to wearing a coat or having anything on their body.

-it requires some work to condition your dog to wearing a backpack if they are to have a positive experience doing so

-It will lose it effectiveness after your dog gets strong enough

PULLING A CART: Some dogs were bred to pull carts in areas where horses couldn't be used. And those dogs truly do seem to love this activity, but not all of them, and only if it is introduced in the right fashion. Often cart pulling is synonymous with weight pulling. Either activity can be made more difficult for the dog with the addition of weight to the sled or cart being pulled. The same issues arise for me with cart pulling as we see with backpacks. But, since there are competitions and a national titling organization, I have to hope that they use ethical and humane guidelines for training and use. Just be sure that it is introduced safely and sanely, and that your dog is comfortable and happy the whole time.

Chapter 6: Training as a Boredom Busters

If you haven't yet taken your dog to a basic obedience class, I have one questions? WHAT ARE YOU WAITING FOR!? But down this book and get online to find yourself a positive reinforcement trainer or better yet, someone in your area who is doing See, Mark, and Reward Training (SMART). Clicker based training is best, so ask around for recommendations on instructors who are Karen Pryor Certified or who are using clickers in class. Check out the resources section at the back of the book to find some places to start your search.

If you are using positive methods, you can teach your dog a million tricks and skills that will not only come in handy, but can be cute and entertaining as well. Dogs love to train and are constantly learning about the world around them.

In an introduction level class, you should learn things like Sit, Down, Come, Loose Leash Walking, etc. Even just doing your homework from that class can help to tire out your pup. It is hard work for them to learn another way to behave and even harder to learn a new language associated with those new behaviors. After a basic class you can go onto Tricks, Agility, Rally-O, Advanced Obedience, Flyball, Nosework, Lure Coursing, Terrier Trials, Treiball, Herding, Schutzhund, Search and Rescue, or make up your own sport!

Even just 10 minutes of learning a new skill each day will help keep your dog's mind active and will also give you a bunch of great behaviors to call upon in moments when you need them!

For some fun videos of ways to train check out www.k9boredombusters.com
-Name Game
-Recall
-Naming of Objects
-101 things to do with a box

A Note: We do not condone punishment based training methods. It is inhumane, ineffective, and bad for your dog's mental state. Please, when you are looking for a trainer, if they ever suggest that you use a prong or pinch collar, a choke chain, or a shock or e-collar walk out of there immediately. Similarly, if they ever kick, hit, pinch, or scare your dog in any manner, or instruct you to do the same, please find another trainer. Your relationship with your dog and the trust your dog places in you as their protector and guardian is too precious to risk on poorly skilled trainers.

Chapter 7: Multiple Dog Households

If I had a dollar for every person who says to me, "I want to adopt a second dog to help tire out my existing dog" I wouldn't be writing this book, I would be relaxing at my villa in Italy. I understand why people think this, I understand why the believe that a second dog will be the answer to all the prayers for a nice tired companion. I understand that those thoughts are often WRONG!

Having one dog who is bored can be annoying, time consuming, stressful, expensive, grating on your nerves. Having two or more dogs that are bored is like living a multi-species version of Lord of the Flies.

Dogs do often play with each other, and help burn off some of some excess sprinter fuel. But they also bump into more furniture, want more time outside, gang up on small animals or scents, pull twice as hard, and team up against you. They will also learn each other's bad habits and tricks. If you have one bored dog, getting a second is likely going to mean that you have two bored dogs.

If you want a second dog, by all means, please, find a suitable second dog, and put in the work to integrate him or her into your home. But be sure you are getting that dog for your enjoyment and happiness as well as the enjoyment and happiness of the other animals and people in the home. Having multiple dogs can be a great blessing and can be endless fun. But for most of us it means twice the toys, twice the attention and effort at feeding time, twice the expense at the vet and the pet supply store. It means twice the walking, and twice the boredom busting.

I have a client who contacted me after she rescued her 4th dog. She had 3 dogs who had been together for several years and got along great. But this 4th dog set off a whirlwind of chaos in the house. He was loud, he was needy, he was demanding of her and the others 3 dogs. Walking 4 dogs all over 60 pounds was a hard task, and none of them were great on a leash due to lack of training. My client thought she was going to have to re-home this new dog because he was such a bad influence over the other dogs. She was struggling to find a system where she could train any of them without the others getting upset. She couldn't get them out for enough walking time to tire anyone out, and she was starting to see the negative effects in the destruction and in-fighting in the house.

I suggested a 2 week trial period where she implemented a SUPER structured boredom buster program. While one dog got a puzzle toy in the spare bedroom, another dog got a toy in the backyard, another was in a crate with a frozen bone, the fourth was in a training session in the kitchen. Then they would rotate. By the end of the 2 hours each evening. All 4 of the dogs had gotten 2 hours of activity. Almost immediately, she saw a big difference. It became even greater when she enlisted the help of her teenaged son to take each dog on a walk as one of the rotations in the evening. He spent 2 hours standing at the end of the leash playing video games or listening to music and the dogs to got sniff and explore the local area to their hearts content, or until it was time to rotate again.

Multi-species Households:
66% of the American population owns a pet, and of those 66% about half own more then one species. So, half of the people with pets have multiple species households. Of course some of those animals live in terrariums, or in tanks, or on a farm. But for some significant percentage there are animals in the home who have to get along or at least not injury each other. Dogs and cats, dog and rabbits, dogs and rats, dogs and guinea pigs, dogs and ferrets, dogs and turtles, dogs and lizards, dogs and birds are the general combinations I deal with. And in most cases they can learn to live peacefully side by side if both species are properly entertained and given enough stimulation. In this case, the dog chasing the cat doesn't count as stimulation. Boredom buster toys exist in great quantities for birds, ferrets, pocket pets, and even fish. They aren't so plentiful for lizards although they don't seem to mind, and the cat market for boredom buster toys is coming along quickly in the last year or

so. And as this book proves there are a million and one ways to enrich your dogs life.

If you go to our website, you will see links to videos of zoo and sanctuary programs for enrichment with a wide variety of "homemade" contraptions to entertain the wild animals in their care. Paper mache gazelles with dinner inside of them for lions and tigers, swinging baskets of fruit for monkeys, puzzle toys for bears and other foragers. If you are creative and have made an enrichment toy for your pet, please feel free to share it on our website!

Rules for Boredom Busting in Multi-dog Households:
I always recommend separating animals for feeding, and boredom busting. It isn't worth the headache and stress to just throw a bunch of valuable resources into the crowd and hope they sort it out so that everyone gets one. It is best to put them in separate rooms or in crates to give them their enrichment toys.
If you would like to play ball with one, then give the other something to do inside.
Many of the things that I recommend as enrichment toys and treats and chews in this book are of high value to the dogs, and having to fight for them or being able to bully each other out of them can cause serious and longterm issues between siblings. Best practices is to keep the dogs on either sides of a sturdy barrier like a door or baby gate when enrichment activities are being handed out.

This also allows you to customize the activities for each dog. And older, fatter dog shouldn't have as many calories or as much fat as a younger more active dog. Older dogs may also have a harder time chewing some of the harder bones or antlers, so be aware that not every enrichment works for every animal.

If you insist that you can't separate your animals or you are 100% sure that they won't steal from each other or bully each other over items, then you must give each dog the same item at the same time. If you are doing this for the first couple of times, it is recommended to have one more identical item then you have dogs, so that if there is a thief or a bully, the victim isn't left with nothing. Sharing isn't easy for dogs, so have extras or put the dogs in their own area to enjoy their toys!

A Word on Cats/Rats/Rabbits/Ferrets: Several of the companies listed in the resources section of the book also make toys either designed for cats or pocket pets or they make sized that are appropriate for smaller animals. Premier specifically makes a line of food dispensing toys for cats, Kong has toys for pocket pets, and ferrets can enjoy a wide variety of the same toys as small dogs or cats.

Chapter 8: Recipes for Successful Stuffing

A word on calories: Dogs in natural environments will scavenge all day or gorge themselves and then not eat for many hours. The conventional wisdom for feeding breakfast, lunch, or dinner to dogs is more a construct of our schedules then anything grounded in biology. So, why not skip dinner in the bowl for your dog and divide his daily food intake between a number of activities and puzzles? If you are going to add enrichment activities with food on top of your dogs regular feedings then be mindful of the number of calories going into your dog. Use the lower calorie recipes and suggestions found in this section.

A word on allergies: Dogs have a long list of things that aren't good for them, some of them will cause some mild stomach upset and loose stool. Other will cause death. Before giving anything new to your dog, please check out the list of toxins on our website or consult your vet. In light of the fact that each dog is sensitive to different things, there is a "Create your own" list at the end of this section that will show you the formula for creating an activity that is both safe and healthy for your pet.

The Learning Curve:
If your dog has never had an enrichment or boredom busting toy they might need some encouragement to work at it until they succeed.

The best way to start a beginner dog, is with a couple of super easy experiences even if they only take the dog a couple of minutes or less. I recommend things like kibble or dry treats that will fall out easily or smearing peanut butter liberally inside the opening of the toy.

After your dog has gotten the hang of working with the toy for a while, then you can start to increase the difficulty. Most dogs will continue to enjoy a bit of easy to access tasty spread at the working end of the toy.

Once your dog is really advanced and not likely to give up when presented with a real challenge you can start to use less valuable objects at the openings of the toys or even block the entrance completely. There is an advanced stuffing recipe that I found online that recommends taking a ravioli or piece of cooked lasagna noodle and putting it inside the opening of a Kong so the dog is represented with a smooth surface to work thru first.

Basic Stuffing:
Layers:
Fill the toy with layers of treats and seal the working end with something soft and tasty. Some suggestions include broken up dog biscuits, kibble, soft dog treats, the peanut butter over the working end of the toy

Filling Mixes: These are purees or mixes of soft foods that completely fill the toy with a uniform product. Canned or even raw dog foods do this really well. These stuffed toys an be used fresh or frozen.

"Jello Salad Style": These stuffings are often crunchy or tasty morsels suspended in another tasty substance. Think of this as a combination option and see the "Catch All Recipe in the frozen section.

Layered or advanced challenges: For my dog, who now eats like this every meal, I am constantly looking for ways to make new and exciting options for him. I have taken to melting cheese in his toys, letting to cool, using a pastry bag to create a thin layer of seal at one end, freezing that, then taking it out and filling it with crunchies and sealing it with more puree and freezing it again. This creates a chamber of food that he can smell and gets excited about but meals he has to work thru the frozen to get to the crunchies he still has the added enjoyment and challenge of cleaning the melted frozen cheese off the sides. Even at his level, this challenge will still occupy him for 30 minutes or so.

Fresh Stuffing: For use immediately

Breakfast buffet:
Grated potato
1 egg,
carrots
shredded cheese or cream cheese

Warm the potato and carrots in a skillet or microwave, add egg and cook until scrambled. Fold in cheese and let cool. Stuff into toy.

Shmere and Lox:
Low fat cream cheese
grated or chopped carrots, broccoli, cauliflower
cooked non-seasoned, deboned salmon with
skin on
Stir veggies into softened creamcheese and
shmear the inside of the toy liberally. Add
salmon, seal the openening with a dog cracker
of cookie

Breakfast Parfait:
Berries
Plain yogurt (unsweetened, flavorless, any fat
content will work)
Dog kibble
Layer Kibble, yogurt, berries, yogurt, and kibble
into the kong.

Salad Bar:
Broccoli
Cauliflower
potato
Carrots
Celery
spinach
kale
sweet potato
Green beans
Puree in a food processor and put into toy

Roll a Meal: Specifically for kibble dispensing
toys, all ingredients are dry.
Dog kibble
freeze dried veggies such as Just Corn or Just
Berries

Freeze dried training treats from Bravo

South Philly:
Left over steak
Cream Cheese
Smear cream cheese into toy, add steak

Microwave Magic:
Put toy into a container to hold it upright. (For most of mine I use a coffee mug)
Add veggies and meat scraps to the toy
Crack and scramble one raw egg and pour it still raw into the toy
Mircrowave for 2 minutes. The egg will expand to fill the toy!
Cool completely before serving!

Superbowl Spread:
Tater tots
cold cuts or left over meat
Cheese
Carrots
Celery
Put Cheese in first and microwave toy to melt cheese to the sides.
Put veggies into the still warm cheese and let cook. Then stuff completely with tater tots and meat into the center of the toy. Be sure it is cooled completely before giving to the dog.

Recipes for Frozen Toys:

Philly Supreme:
Left over Steak (no onions)
Cream Cheese
Green beans
Puree green beans, cream cheese. Add Steak and stuff into toy. Freeze for 3 hours before feeding

Holiday Fete:
Butternut Squash or pumpkin cooked
blueberries
spinach
turkey or chicken meat
green beans
Layer spinach, blueberries, squash, and turkey, put green beans in last and leave the ends sticking out of the toy. Freeze for 2 hours before feeding.

Easter Egger:
Hardboiled egg
Rabbit flavored canned dog food
Pineapple
slice the egg and layer it with pineapple and canned dog food inside the toy. If you are stuffing for a big dog, you can leave the egg whole and stuff pineapple and canned food around it. Freeze for 2 hours before feeding

Hunting Season:
Rabbit or Venison flavored dog food
Freeze dried veggies such as Just Corn or Just Peas
Beef jerky
Mix freeze dried veggies into canned dog food and stuff into toy. Insert beef jerky and leave ends sticking out of toy. Freeze for 3 hours before feeding

Sashimi boat:
Fish flavored dog food
kale or spinach
left over cooked and cooled rice
Layer Kale (to create a seal over one end), then dog food, then rice. Fill toy with broth, set upright in container and freeze for 5 hours before serving
Sake Bombs:
Large Leaves of napa cabbage or other large leaf lettuce
Cooked left over meat or canned dog food
Crunchy dog biscuits or left over dog treats
Instant Mashed potatos made with meat broth or canned sweet potato

Mix wet and dry ingredients together and roll up inside the cabbage leaves. The leaves are made more pliable by steaming or a quick trip thru the microwave with a damp papertowel. Roll the food mixture up into the leaves and freeze. They are a ton of fun dropped into a doggie pool or water dish, or just given as a frozen snack!

Catch All: (I keep a tupperware container in my fridge and anytime I am making dinner I put all my dog-safe veggies scraps in there. At least once a week I can use those carrot peels and left over broccoli steams to make this recipe)

Veggie scraps (NO ONIONS)

instant potato flakes

Cheese or meat scraps as available.

I mix the food scraps together with the dry potato flakes and then add chick stock until I like the consistency. This is a very different recipe each time so I change the potato to stock recipe each time. I want it to be glue-like but with about 50% food scraps to potato. Stuff into toys, (I especially like this one for hooves, and bones) and freeze for 4 hours.

Create your own:

Crunchies:
Dog Kibble
Freeze Dried Raw Dog Kibble
Freeze Dried Raw Patties
Dog Biscuits
Dog Cookies
Plain air popped popcorn

Freshies:
Carrots
Broccoli
Cabbage

Boredom Busters - www.k9boredombusters.com

Cauliflower
Parsnips
Potatoes
Sweet Potatoes
Kale
Spinach
Collards
Tomatoes
Blueberries
Strawberries
Squash (All kinds)
Peas
Banana
apple
pear
pineapple
Cranberries

Proteins:
Fish
Chicken
Beef
pork
venison
lamb/mutton
rabbit
other poultry
other livestock
other wild animals
eggs
cheese

Chewies:
Beef Jerky
Chewy dog treats such as Soft and Chewy
Buddy Biscuits, Zukes, or Real Meat treats

Dehydrated fruit or veggies such as sweet
potato chews and homemade fruit leather)

Liquids:
Chick/beef/pork/fish broth (NO ONIONS)
Apple Sauce
Water
Yogurt

Binders:
Cream Cheese
Peanut Butter
Canned Sweet Potato
Canned Pumpkin Puree
Instant Mashed Potatoes
Cheese
Eggs

Chapter 9: Resources

www.K9Boredombusters.com
 -We have a great list of items you can buy directly from our website. We also have links to places where you can order the items we can't provide online.

www.amazon.com
- A great catch all for all manners of boredom buster toys. And you can sometimes find amazing deals.

www.bravorawdiet.com
 -We love love love their raw food, bully sticks, and freeze dried training treats. They have a search feature on their website that allows you to find local retailers that carry their products.

www.Premier.com
- They have a great line of interactive toys for dogs, cats, ferrets, and birds. They also make our favorite walking harness The Easy Walk.

www.kong.com
 -You need their products. And their website has some great recipes and useful tips on using all of their product lines efficiently and best. I don't love their treats and canned stuffings.

www.vitalessentialsraw.com
-If you want to feed your dog raw, but don't want to have to deal with defrosting food each day for your dog, you really need to look into the freeze dried kibble that they produce. They are a great size for making food dispensing toys harder but more rewarding to advanced dogs! They also make a freeze dried patty that makes a great training treat.

www.Stellandchewys.com
 -This company produces one of the most palatable freeze dried raw diets I have ever seen. I use their regular diet in my training all the time since I don't feed my dog from a bowl. They also make a great line of training treats. Easy to break up, and really good and smelly to the dogs!

www.clickertraining.com
- Find Clicker trainers in your area who have passed the schools rigorous program. They also offer articles, videos, books, and equipment to help you get started with training.

www.ingramcontent.com/pod-product-compliance
Lightning Source LLC
Chambersburg PA
CBHW031226090426
42740CB00007B/722